Right Before Your Eyes

A Fresh Approach to Interpreting a Piano Score

BY RUTH PRICE

Edited by Jennifer Linn

Back cover photo: by Jerry Naunheim Photography

ISBN 978-1-4803-6403-5

HAL•LEONARD® CORPORATION

7777 W. BLUEMOUND RD. P.O. BOX 13819 MILWAUKEE, WI 53213

In Australia Contact:
Hal Leonard Australia Pty. Ltd.
4 Lentara Court
Cheltenham, Victoria, 3192 Australia
Email: ausadmin@halleonard.com.au

Visit Hal Leonard Online at
www.halleonard.com

For my parents

TABLE OF CONTENTS

ACKNOWLEDGEMENTS

This book would not have been possible without the support from many wonderful people. I would like to thank my teachers Michael Coonrod, Lee Luvisi, Gyorgy Sebok, and Gilbert Kalish for years of inspiration; my editor, Jennifer Linn, for her support and guidance; all the cheerleaders among friends and family: John McGrosso, Jane Price, Kurt Baldwin, Melissa Brooks, Pauline Lee, Dan Rubright, Leslie Peters, Billie Derham, Bob and Gail Melson, my daughter, Lucy, and of course, my colleagues from Webster University; my first class of piano literature students, whose enthusiasm helped me develop as a teacher; Pat Eastman, Donna Vince, Karl Koesterer, and Mark Spurrier, who listened to me bounce around ideas; my piano students for coming with me on this quest to find magic in a piece; and my parents for first exposing me to classical music, and for teaching me to value the art of writing.

And my mother, Lillian, who always wants to analyze why she likes something.

INTRODUCTION

When I was a college student, my piano teacher told me that score study was an important part of practicing. I didn't think of asking him how to do it. I just took my score of Beethoven Opus 7 and walked it over to the couch. I stared at it for a while, but that was about as far as I got.

But the truth is, I did want a deeper understanding of music. For instance, I had recently heard the late Schubert sonatas for the first time, and I wanted to take them apart and look for what I now call "the magic": the compositional elements that give a piece its identity. Although I was taking analysis classes, I was still just collecting tools and terminology. I had not yet found an approach that I could make my own. I realize now that what I was looking for was a way of integrating score study with those great listening experiences. **I wanted to use my emotional reaction to the music as a place to begin analytical thinking.**

The turning point came the first time I taught a college piano literature class. After spending most of the first semester discussing sonata forms, we arrived at 19th century character pieces. I knew I had to take a different approach with this music. So I told the class that the creation of a character or mood was a priority for composers of this period. I brought out the Chopin E minor prelude and asked them to describe the character. Confidently they offered words like "dreamy" and "introspective". Then I asked them, "What do you see in the music that creates that character?" They looked at me blankly and began to chuckle at the sudden silence in the room. At that moment I knew what I had to do. Whether it was a short Chopin piece or one by Mendelssohn, Schumann or Brahms, I kept asking them the same question: "What specifically did the composer do to create that character?" They started to get better at it, and later, most of them said it was their favorite part of the class.

The more I taught this way, the more this kind of questioning got me closer to the music I was practicing myself. I started applying this approach to composers of all periods. Eventually I would routinely ask myself three questions: what is the character, how is it created, and what does this imply for my interpretation? These three steps take me from my emotional response, through objective score exploration, and finally to an interpretation that evolves from both. I finally had a way of getting inside the music.

Once I realized how much this basic method was helping me, as well as my students, I began looking for other ways into a score. Where are the surprises in the music? How can I get more comfortable with transitions? How does score study affect my choice of tempo? How does phrase-length influence my interpretation? This book is the result of that search which I hope will continue throughout my life as a musician.

Using these techniques has revolutionized the way I teach and interpret music. I have been surprised that these tools can be adapted even for students at early levels. With a little guidance, even students who know almost no theory can gain a deeper understanding of their pieces. There is quite a big side benefit for teachers, too: when a student hasn't learned a piece well enough yet to play through it, instead of using the lesson time to slog through the learning process that should have been done at home, teacher and student can analyze the piece together, generating infinitely more fun and discovery for both of them.

Not only do these techniques help me figure out why I love certain passages, but they also help me with the parts that I have trouble relating to, such as awkward transitions or places where the music seems to lose direction. In the chapter called "I Hate This Part", I will share how I became more comfortable, musically and physically, with a few such passages through score study. When I feel comfortable, then I am free to be musical. But I cannot feel comfortable without knowing what I want to say with the music.

Of course, it is quite possible for talented performers to play musically even before they study the score. Any score study that follows may simply show them the reason that they are already playing in a particular way, which is satisfying in itself.

Teaching, however, can never rely simply on instinct: otherwise we will be saying, "take time here, crescendo there" without giving the student solid reasons. The student will remain dependent on the teacher, and will never learn the art of interpretation.

About the different methods

The purpose of each method in this book is to provide an immediate entrance into the score that helps us gather information. Each method provides a starting place that leads to knowledge broader than the method itself; in other words, if I study phrase-length, I will inevitably learn more about the piece than just the length of the phrases. If I study character, there is no limit to the musical topics that could come up. I encourage the reader, therefore, to enter into each chapter with the faith that a broader landscape of the piece will come to light than the title of the chapter might suggest.

*Toward the end of the discussion of each piece, I present my suggestions for interpretation. The reader should know, however, that the primary focus of the book is on the interpretation **processes** rather than on my specific performance ideas.*

As for the musical examples, I chose only very well-known pieces for two reasons: first, so that they would be familiar to most pianists; secondly, because these are the pieces that don't surprise us anymore. We need to revisit them in order to discover why we fell in love with them in the first place.

Using this book

This book should be read at the piano so that the reader can play the examples. Some examples are short passages that I have rewritten in a more predictable or square style in order to highlight the beauty of the original work. I particularly recommend playing these "square" versions so that they can be compared to the original passages.

On the college level, this book can be used as a supplement to piano pedagogy and analysis classes. For the private studio it can provide new insights for the teacher, as well as material that can be adapted for students of different levels. For any pianist, it can be a companion book for inspiration, as well as a resource for increasing confidence on stage. A common cause of stage-fright is the feeling that somehow we do not belong on the stage; we do not measure up. But when the focus is on what we want to communicate in the music, rather than on our perceived limitations, we can become much more comfortable. Score study is an excellent way to find that focus.

Finally, this book is for all of us who feel a pang of longing when listening to beautiful music. I believe that, at least in part, this longing comes from the urge to be at one with the music, and from the desire to know more about why we love it.

PART 1

Easy Entrances to the Score

CHAPTER 1
The Three-Step Method

What makes the opening of Beethoven's Sonata Op. 2, No. 1 so exciting? And how do we study the score to develop an interpretation?

Fig. 1.1. Beethoven, Sonata, Op. 2, No. 1.

Here is one of the methods I use to get started. For each passage I ask three questions:

Step 1: What is the character?

Step 2: What in the score creates that character?

Step 3: What does this imply for my interpretation?

These three steps provide a smooth entrance into the score. Let's try them now on the opening of Op. 2, no. 1.

Step 1: What is the character?

The answer to this question is brief and subjective. We don't think much. We use only our initial reaction to the music. For me, *nervous energy* comes to mind: Nervous energy…*with uncertainty and surprises.*

Step 2: How does Beethoven create this character?

This second step is no longer subjective; it is time for fact-finding in the score. The very opening measures have *energy* because of the charging "rocket" motive and the fast triplets; but what I find more interesting is that the *nervousness* comes from the absence of accompaniment, as well as the delay of a strong downbeat. The meter is not established until the downbeat of bar 3. Of course for some of us, the piece is so familiar that we are not actually confused when we listen to it; but imagine Beethoven's audience hearing it for the first time; the very first note could sound like the downbeat. I suggest comparing Beethoven's opening to the following version to which I have added a simple accompaniment:

Fig. 1.2. My version with added accompaniment, Op. 2, No. 1.

In my version there is no doubt about the meter. Comparing these two versions helps me appreciate the uncertainty of Beethoven's opening. Although the opening arpeggiated "rocket" motive was a common musical tradition of the day, a rocket motive was usually supported by a strong downbeat, as in Beethoven's Opus 10, No.1, for example:

Fig. 1.3. Beethoven, Sonata, Op. 10, No. 1.

Both opening themes feature rockets, but Op. 2, No. 1 sounds more agitated, while Op. 10, No. 1 is more declamatory, largely due to this rhythmic difference.

Let's look now at the *surprises* beginning in bar 5. We might have expected the melodic pattern to continue rocketing up to a high C, and we certainly don't expect the sudden lyricism at the end of the phrase. I like to imagine what a lesser composer might have written without the surprises:

Fig. 1.4. My version without the surprises, Op. 2, No. 1, bars 1-8.

But instead of continuing to the high C, Beethoven steps back to A-flat (bar 5), beginning the ascent to C once again. He condenses the 2- bar material from the opening into single bars by shortening the rocket to a single grace note. This creates a stretto effect (an acceleration), increasing the *nervous energy*.

Fig. 1.5. Op. 2, No. 1, bars 5-8.

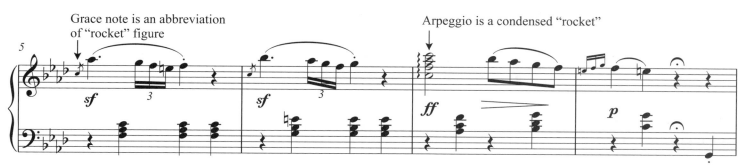

Sforzandos add to the agitation, until finally we arrive at the high C in bar 7. At this climax, suddenly the melody becomes more lyrical, and the meter is obscured again due to the rhythmic change in the accompaniment. Once again there is a feeling of *uncertainty*; the last chord before the fermata comes on a weak beat and the leading tone in the melody is left hanging. As a result, bars 7 and 8 sound improvised, momentarily stepping out of the driving momentum.

If we play my version without the surprises and then play the original, we can appreciate the intensity of the stretto, and the strange ending before the fermata.

Step 3: How can all this apply to interpretation?
The answers here are once again subjective, but based on observations from step 2.

To bring out the *uncertainty* in bars 1-4, it is crucial to avoid accenting the first downbeat, so as to keep the meter a secret. To emphasize the first clear downbeat (bar3), we can crescendo with the left hand chords, which will sound agitated in contrast to the natural tapering of the melody in bar 2.

We should also make only enough crescendo in the first rocket as is necessary for shaping, saving the emphasis for the *sforzando* in bar 5.

Fig. 1.6. My interpretation, Op. 2, No. 1 bars 1-4.

In bars 5-8, to show the *surprises* the *sforzandos* should sound jarring. Then at the climax in bar 7 we should take time because first of all, the theme becomes suddenly lyrical, and secondly, those eighth notes form an augmented version of the triplet motive—and augmentation implies broadening. The rolled chord, by contrast is a condensed version of the rocket; so in that single measure we have diminution and augmentation side by side, creating great intensity.

Fig. 1.7. Op. 2, No. 1, bars 7-8.

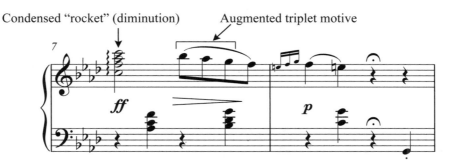

To show *uncertainty* I suggest playing more freely in bars 7-8 to emphasize the obscured meter and the feeling of improvisation.

Fig. 1.8. My interpretation of bars 5-8, Op. 2, No. 1.

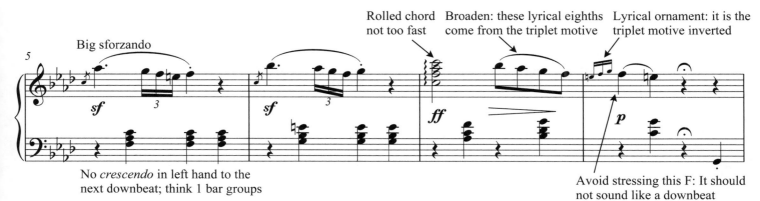

I studied this piece as a student but never thought about the absence of bass at the opening. I also never considered that the unpredictability of the rhythm was crucial to the identity of this theme. I probably just focused on articulation and dynamics without going deeper into the score to find out what was really going on. But now, having this method, I am challenged to think about more than just musical gestures and traditions; I now know that there are ways to get in touch with why I love the music.

Let's try the three-step method now with music of a different style: the middle section of Chopin's Fantasie-Impromptu.

Fig. 1.9. Chopin, Fantasie-Impromptu, Op. 66, bars 41-48.

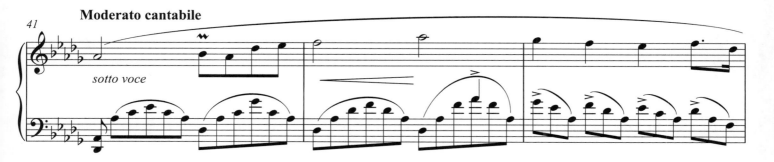

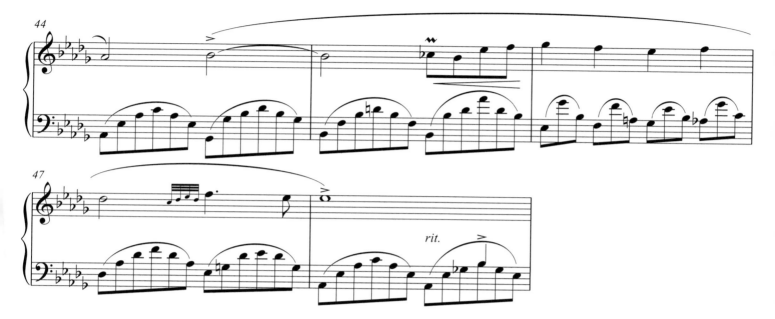

Everybody melts at the sound of this melody. Almost a century after it was composed, it was made into the popular song "I'm Always Chasing Rainbows" (adapted by Harry Carroll, lyrics by Joseph McCarthy, introduced in the Broadway show "Oh Look!" in 1918). Why is this theme so irresistible?

Step 1: What is the character?

Again, this is subjective. I came up with *unabashedly romantic,* which is a shorter way of saying *"youthfully warm and passionate, with freedom and some urgency"*.

Step 2: What makes it *unabashedly romantic*?

First there are some obvious answers: the large range of the melody, combined with the soaring shape of the phrase provides *warmth,* as does the expansive legato accompaniment. But more interesting is **the early entrance of the second phrase on the third beat of bar 44.** This early entrance creates a feeling of *urgency and passion*. It also makes the melody seamless, saving the theme from a square 4 + 4 bar phrase structure. Instead, Chopin has created a more fluid 3½ + 4½ bar structure.

In fact, now that we are discussing phrase structure, these two phrases are not only different in length; they are also different rhythmically. Imagine if these phrases were parallel in design:

Fig. 1.10. My parallel version of the theme, Fantasie-Impromptu, bars 41-48.

My parallel version takes away the wonderful flexibility Chopin achieves when he presents the rhythms of the second phrase in a different order. With that flexibility, Chopin adds fluidity and freedom to the soaring shape of the melody:

Fig. 1.11 Chopin presents the rhythm of the second phrase in a different order, Fantasie-Impromptu, bars 41-48.

So we are discovering that the variety in the phrase structure creates a flow and seamlessness that contributes to a feeling of freedom. Let's look at one more difference between the two phrases: Chopin's changes to the accompaniment in the second phrase. Notice that the first phrase begins with two measures of D-flat pedal point; then in bar 43 the bass seems to drop out and the tenor voice is the leader.

Fig. 1.12. Bassline movement, Fantasie-Impromptu, bars 41-44.

Now compare the accompaniment in the first phrase to that of the second phrase, which begins with surprising root position harmonies instead of a pedal point, and continues in bar 46 with a strong bassline instead of the floating tenor melody.

Fig. 1.13. Bassline movement, Fantasie-Impromptu, bars 44-48.

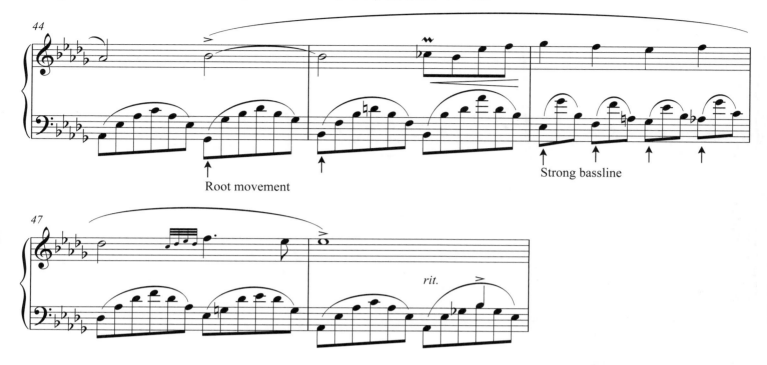

Both of these differences add to the variety that keeps this very diatonic melody interesting and fluid. This fluidity is an important factor in the feeling of *freedom* and expansiveness; a 4+4 bar structure would feel more confined.

There is one more event that creates some *urgency*: in bar 47 we think we've arrived at a full cadence, but Chopin impulsively shifts to a half cadence mid-bar as if to prevent the soaring melody from settling down to earth, providing even more continuity of line.

We have discussed what makes the melody romantic, but what about *unabashedly*? That word implies that the romanticism is heart-on-sleeve, or youthfully idealistic. What in the score produces that? I think it is the combination of innocence, exuberance and impulsiveness. The innocence can be found in the diatonicism and triadic nature of the tune; the exuberance in the fact that Chopin lingers ecstatically on the highest notes of the phrase; and the impulsiveness in the two surprises: the early entrance of the second phrase and the change to the half cadence.

Step 3: What does this imply for my interpretation?

In performance we must respond to the differences between the two phrases, the lush warmth of the melody, and the early entrance of the second phrase. We also need to bring out the surprising change to a half cadence in bar 47. *How* we respond is subjective, and may vary with each repetition of the theme. Here are some possible interpretive ideas:

Fig. 1.14. My interpretation, Fantasie-Impromptu, bars 41-48.

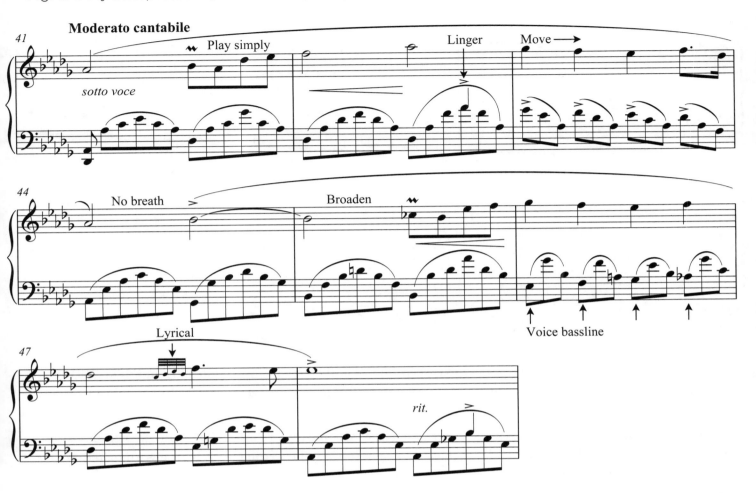

In bars 41 and 42 we should play simply and steadily due to the pedal point stability and the diatonic simplicity of the melody. At the end of bar 42, we can linger on the entrance of the tenor voice, and then move forward in bar 43 with the faster note values in the melody.

To emphasize the early entrance of the second phrase, we can omit a musical breath before the B-flat on beat 3 of bar 44. Then we can broaden the first half of bar 45 to emphasize the length of the tied melody note, as well as to dwell on the surprising root position harmonies. In bar 46 we should voice out the new bassline. I suggest playing the ornament in bar 47 lyrically and freely in order to highlight the change from the full cadence to the half cadence.

It seems miraculous that despite all of his attention to detail and variation, Chopin is still able to make this melody sound simple and natural. He has written a tune that is so repetitive and diatonic that the listener is not conscious of the variation that creates so much beauty.

Notice that starting with character took us into a study of the melodic and rhythmic structure of this theme. From there we pondered how to bring out the seamless flexibility of the melody in performance. The three-step method, then, is just a starting point that can lead to surprising results; **and this was only eight bars**! Much more can be gained by studying a whole piece this way, section by section. This method requires a combination of left and right brain activity, which I believe leads a musician to a deeper connection to the music.

CHAPTER 2
Phrases of Odd Lengths:
Beauty, Humor, and Passion

Sometimes the unusual length of a phrase can be the secret to its beauty. For a very simple but rewarding method of score study, we can look through a piece for any phrase that does not have a standard 2, 4, 8, or 16-bar structure. Once we find a phrase with an odd length, we can ask questions like, *What is the effect on the listener? How can I bring this out in my interpretation? How would the phrase have sounded with a more standard length?*

Let's try out this method with Schubert's Impromptu Op. 90, No. 1:

Fig. 2.1. Schubert, Impromptu, Op. 90, No. 1 (D.899), bars 1-9.

The entire first section of this piece is made up of 4-bar phrases that seem to be intentionally square and symmetrical, often marchlike in character. By contrast, the first five-bar phrase soars with astonishing freedom:

Fig. 2.2. Schubert, Op. 90, No. 1, bars 42-46.

The odd length is easy to overlook because of the more obvious changes of key and texture. The change in phrase-length is more subtle: the extra bar seems to be bar 44; if we take it away the phrase still makes sense. No other bar in the phrase is expendable. Imagine the phrase without bar 44:

Fig. 2.3. My 4-bar version of Schubert, Op. 90, No. 1, bars 42-46.

This 4-bar version is acceptable as a musical thought—but when we bring back bar 44 we can appreciate its magical effect: it delays the cadence we expect, and that delay creates a feeling of suspended time. It is like a momentary glimpse of the infinite.

Schubert enhances this feeling of suspended time by adding suspensions in the accompaniment:

Fig. 2.4. Schubert Op. 90, No. 1, bars 43-44, showing suspensions.

These suspensions create poignant dissonances as well as a lingering effect, contributing to the tenderness of this moment.

Now that we have noticed these features, how can we apply them to interpretation? If we want to communicate that timeless feeling, we should play measure 44 with a lack of direction. We can let it float; in other words, take a little time.

Fig. 2.5. My interpretation, Schubert, Op. 90, No. 1, bars 42-46.

I recommend playing the square 4-bar version once again, and then playing the original, taking time in bar 44. Hearing a banal version can be an eye-opening experience even for the lay person. For a musician it can provide the key to interpreting a passage convincingly.

The Schubert melody is an example of an unusual phrase-length creating *beauty*. Now let's look at a piece in which odd phrase-lengths create *humor*: the third movement of Haydn's Sonata in C (Hob. XVI/50).

Fig. 2.6. Haydn, Sonata in C, Hob. XVI/50, third movement, bars 1-24.

The humor of this movement comes largely from the asymmetry of the phrase structures. The opening consists of a 10-bar group, divided into 7 bars plus 3 bars. The 3-bar phrase is especially funny because it ends so abruptly on that startling B Major chord.

Then after a typical Haydn silence, the C Major theme starts over, ignoring the B Major chord as if to say, "Just kidding!" The asymmetry continues: the next phrase is surprisingly longer (12 bars), including 4 extra bars that delay the cadence (bars 19-22). Imagine that same phrase without those four bars:

Fig. 2.7. My shortened version of Haydn Hob. XVI/50, III, beginning in bar 12.

This shorter version is more predictable. But those extra bars provide the humor and momentum. So what is going on in those four measures?

First of all, the fragmenting of the right hand material produces an acceleration effect: instead of:

Fig. 2.8. Haydn, Hob. XVI/50, III, bars 18-19.

We get:

Fig. 2.9. Haydn, Hob. XVI/50, III, bars 20-21.

Secondly, these extra bars feature descending thirds in the left hand:

Fig. 2.10. Haydn, Hob. XVI/50, III, bars 19-22.

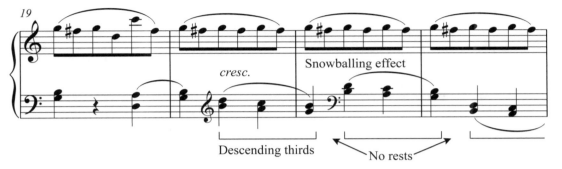

that are compressed compared to the earlier rising thirds in the piece:

Fig. 2.11. Haydn, Hob. XVI/50, III, bars 4-7.

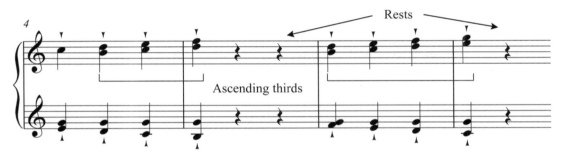

In these extra bars, not only do the thirds descend, but they come one right after another without the rests in between that we heard in bars 4-8. This acceleration creates a snowballing effect to the cadence.

There is also humor in the character change from the dainty right hand thirds in bars 4-7 to these rambunctious, tumbling thirds in bars 19-22. Finally, the surprising extra length of this passage is funny in itself; considering the playfulness of the character, with the extra length, the passage seems to mock its own self-importance.

So how does all this affect interpretation? First of all, to bring out this feeling of acceleration, we should show the difference between the light, bouncy, playful material:

Fig. 2.12. Haydn, Hob. XVI/50, III, bars 12-16.

and the accelerating, rambunctious material:

Fig. 2.13. Haydn, Hob. XVI/50, III, bars 20-24.

We can hold on to the tempo in the bouncy music and push forward in the accelerating passages.

Secondly, we need to emphasize the abrupt silences that create humor:

Fig. 2.14. Haydn, Hob. XVI/50, III, bars 10-12.

And finally, we should bring out the thirds in the left hand at the beginning now that we know they are thematic:

Fig. 2.15. Haydn, Hob. XVI/50, III, bars 1-7.

In addition to beauty and humor, unusual phrase-lengths can also create passion and intensity, as in the first theme of Mozart's Sonata in A minor, K. 310.

Fig. 2.16. Mozart, Sonata in A Minor, K. 310.

The first phrase group is five bars long, and the material is strangely repetitive and insistent. What if Mozart had written a more symmetrical phrase structure in four bars?

Fig. 2.17. My 4-bar version of Mozart, K. 310, opening.

This version is much less dramatic because it is predictable.

The asymmetry continues as the theme unfolds: next is a group of only three bars that are violently interrupted by a return of the opening material.

How can we communicate this strange asymmetry in performance? First of all, we need to bring out the stubborn repetition and sustained intensity of the first five bars. To do that I avoid shaping the melody dynamically in the first phrase, to show its stubbornness. Then in the 3-bar group I shape and taper each gesture to emphasize the short length. Finally, I resist the temptation to crescendo into the forte interruption in bar 9; that way I can emphasize the clipped length of the three-bar group.

Fig. 2.18. My interpretation, Mozart, K. 310, bars 1-10.

Once again, a simple method of score study yields more than its topic implies. In these three examples we set out to examine phrase length, but we found ourselves looking at texture, character, harmony, and surprise. Any doorway into the score, no matter how plain it might seem, is worth entering.

CHAPTER 3
Surprises

By the time I have practiced a piece enough that it is fairly well learned, the unpredictable moments that might have surprised me at first have become familiar. Moreover, if it is a very well-known piece, I may already be used to the surprises even before I begin working on it. This presents an opportunity for score study: to go through a piece and find all the unpredictable moments: not just obvious surprises, but any interesting change of pattern in the rhythm, pitches, harmonic rhythm, phrase length, and so on.

I find this technique especially useful with pieces from the Classical era in which the surprises are more subtle than in later repertoire. Let's take the first theme from Mozart's Sonata in F Major, K. 332 as an example.

Fig. 3.1. Mozart, Sonata in F Major, K. 332, bars 1-12.

Before I studied the score I noticed only the lyricism of the melody, and the counterpoint in the second phrase. I never really appreciated the surprise in bars 5 and 6: that the accompaniment suddenly drops out. That is interesting for several reasons.

First of all, we have had strong downbeats in the first 4 bars. Now we hear 2 bars as one unit, and the change in pulse makes bars 5 and 6 float. Secondly, notice the pitches in those 2 bars. The way they are arranged in pairs hints at hemiola. What might this passage have sounded like with a more standard rhythm? Here is a possible version:

Fig. 3.2. My version of Mozart, K. 332, bars 5-6, without surprises.

But Mozart places the high note on the *second* beat of bar 6, rather than the first, and adds a dot, encouraging the pianist to linger slightly on that C.

Fig. 3.3. Mozart, K. 332, bars 5-6, showing hemiola.

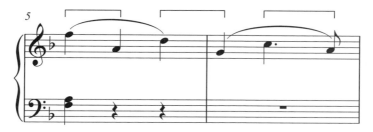

The pulse becomes clear again in bar 8 because of the emphasis on the downbeat in the right hand. I always liked that suspension, but I never knew there was more to it than just the harmonic beauty; that it was an important *rhythmic* moment.

Fig. 3.4. Mozart, K. 332, bars 7-8.

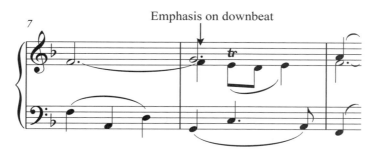

The absence of accompaniment in bars 5 and 6 also serves to emphasize the entrance of counterpoint in bar 7. It is like the beginning of a little fugue.

Just this one surprise can affect interpretation. To bring out the soaring effect in bars 5 and 6, we need to avoid stressing the downbeat of bar 6, so that 5 and 6 will sound suspended and the hemiola will be heard. Then we can lean into the downbeat of bar 8 with the treble voices as a rhythmic contrast to the hemiola in the bass.

As for the overall pacing, we should move the tempo in the first 4 bars to show the flowing accompaniment, and hold back bars 5 and 6 by comparison. Then we can move again in bar 7 to show the flow of the counterpoint.

Fig. 3.5. My interpretation, Mozart, K. 332, bars 1-12.

Of course this kind of flexibility when playing Mozart is subtle. But what is not subtle is the difference in *how I feel* playing the music with that kind of awareness. It is the feeling of knowing what I'm doing.

This method works for any style. In Clair de lune, for example, Debussy leaves a lot of interpretive decisions to the pianist. His only dynamic marking for the first 12 measures is "pianissimo, con sordina"; yet he also writes "tres expressif." So how are we going to be expressive in this passage while staying so soft? I believe the answer lies in bringing out the subtle surprises or what I will call "changes".

Fig. 3.6. Debussy, Clair de lune, from Suite Bergamasque, bars 1-14.

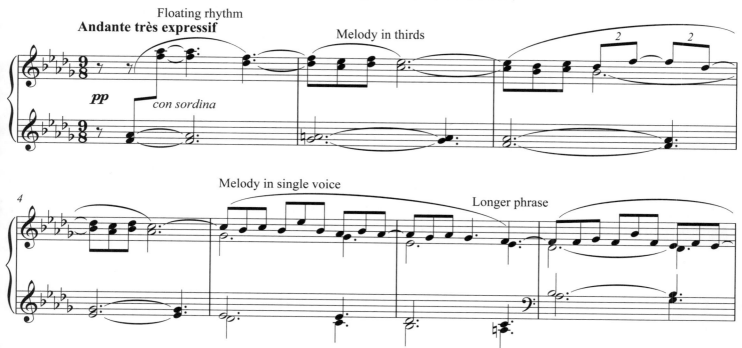

Strong root position downbeat

The moonlight that opens the piece is hazy, as if from behind clouds. The haze is created partly by the vague, floating rhythm; the piece begins on an offbeat, and continues with frequent ties over barlines. The texture of the melody in thirds also contributes to this haziness, as if the tune is out of focus. The first change happens in bar 3, and especially in bar 5 when the thirds switch to single notes. These moments hint to the pianist to produce a somewhat clearer, more penetrating sound. It is as if we had been seeing double through binoculars (thirds) and then focused them (single notes).

Another change happens in bar 5: a longer phrase, four bars instead of two. Getting a more focused sound here will also help give this longer phrase linear direction.

The next change occurs in bar 9: we have our first root position chord. Up until then we only had inversions, which contributed to the floating character. This restatement of the theme begins on a downbeat this time, which, combined with the root position gives us a reason to get a deeper more solid sound here. Clearly Debussy wants more sound, because he writes the melody in octaves in the next few bars. Therefore, we need to think of the opening pianissimo as a mood, rather than a literal dynamic that applies to the whole section. Our gradations of volume can happen within a relatively soft dynamic, but we must feel free to move in and out of pianissimo in order to communicate these changes.

Chopin's Prelude in E minor presents a challenge similar to Clair de lune: eight measures with only "piano" indicated at the beginning; and in this case, the material has a sameness that makes interpretation difficult. How do we shape the first 8 bars? Again, this music is so familiar to some of us that we need to study the score to notice what is unpredictable.

The secret lies in the harmonic rhythm. Notice that there is only one harmony in the first bar, but there are two in the second, and three in the third and fourth bars. After that the harmonic rhythm gradually slows again. Once we notice this, we can shape the phrase with a swell to the downbeat of bar 5, at which time the harmonic rhythm begins to slow down.

Fig. 3.7. Chopin, Prelude, Op. 28, No. 4, harmonic rhythm.

Before I noticed the swell in the harmonic rhythm, I was puzzled about how to shape the phrase; I knew it was all about harmony, but all the harmonies were beautiful. It was impossible to find the harmonic peak until I realized that it was not the harmonies themselves, but the rate at which they changed, that required my attention.

Looking for surprises can reveal intriguing new information, or it can simply steer us back to our original excitement about a piece. We can also discover the reasons behind our natural interpretive impulses. No matter what we learn, we become more conscious of the musical elements that give the piece life.

CHAPTER 4
Your Favorite Part

One easy way to study a score is to start with your favorite part of the piece. You can trust you ear; if it is your favorite spot there is probably a good reason; and when you figure out why it is your favorite spot, it usually leads to some solid information about the piece. For this chapter I will use a short student piece so that we can quickly see how the favorite part relates to the piece as a whole.

Fig. 4.1. C.P.E. Bach, Polonaise, H. 1, No. 4.

My favorite moment in this C.P.E. Bach Polonaise has always been bar 11. It is so joyful and exuberant compared to the serious opening. So I start by simply asking what's so special about that measure?

It is special because it is not the material we expect. What we expect is a transposition of bar 3:

Fig. 4.2. My predictable version of C.P.E. Bach, Polonaise, bar 11

But instead he writes:

Fig. 4.3. C.P.E. Bach, Polonaise, bar 11, original version.

In bar 11 there is a syncopation resulting in an accent in the left hand on beat 2.

The other surprise is the texture: the right hand thirds come in at the beginning of the bar this time.

Starting with this bar eventually led me to see that the strength of this piece is the way Bach varies the rhythm and texture. He sets up an expectation and then writes something different.

Here is another example of varied texture: notice that at the beginning of the piece the texture is stark:

Fig. 4.4. C.P.E. Bach, Polonaise, bars 1-2.

We have the same melodic line in both hands. That creates a bold statement. Notice how that changes in bar 13:

Fig. 4.5. C.P.E. Bach, Polonaise, bars 13-14.

The harmony is filled in with thirds and we now have a bassline. It is a sweeter sound, which inspires me to play more legato there.

The rhythm beginning in m. 13 is also is interesting: the ties and the left hand 16ths provide flow over the barlines, as opposed to the opening bars in which the action stops on the third beats. The other difference beginning in bar 13 is that the stress is on the first beat instead of the third beat, as in the opening bars.

In bar 17 Bach changes the texture and rhythm again.

Fig. 4.6. C.P.E. Bach, Polonaise, bars 17-18.

The character here is very different from the opening. It is more linear and flowing, because instead of the same line in both hands we now have counterpoint. And look at the rhythm: instead of stopping on the third beat as he does at the beginning, the left hand continues the right hand's rhythm on the third beat. Remember, stopping on the third beat was the trademark of this piece! Notice also how the left hand in bar 17 is tied over to the next bar; whereas in the opening, the first two bars are clearly separate.

So interpretively, in bar 17 we need to bring out the linear quality of the left hand, and particularly the third beat moving forward to the next bar.

The accents in bar 17 are back to the third beats. But then in bars 19 and 20 there is no strong beat because of the tie in the right hand in bar 19, and the uninterrupted 16ths in bar 20; without any strong beats, these 16ths drive to the return of the theme in bar 21. So as an interpreter not only do I need to notice accents, but I also need to notice the *absence* of accents.

Fig. 4.7. C.P.E. Bach, Polonaise, bars 19-21.

To summarize, I started with my favorite part, bar 11, knowing only that it was exuberant. From there, I discovered what material was actually expected in that measure. That led to a study of rhythm and texture throughout the piece, and a much better understanding of the identity and pacing of the piece as a whole.

CHAPTER 5
"I Hate This Part!"
(Or, Zen and the Art of the Awkward Passage)

In the previous chapters I've been talking about discovering the magic in particularly beautiful musical passages. But what about those awkward moments in a piece? Sometimes I notice that I am just trying to survive playing those sections in order to get to the next beautiful part. But this is what I have discovered: usually I am uncomfortable because *I am fighting the true nature of that passage,* and that is why it is awkward for me. The reason I use the word "Zen" is that instead of fighting the nature of the passage, I need to embrace it as it is. And in order to do that, I have to decide what I think the passage is about.

Haydn, Sonata in B-flat, Hob. XVI/41

This is a piece that I have always loved, except for one passage: the transition to the recapitulation, consisting mainly of chromatic scales:

Fig. 5.1. Haydn, Sonata in B-flat, Hob. XVI/41, first movement, bars 85-90.

I couldn't find the music in it. There is no melody, and I couldn't find anything interesting about the rhythm or harmony. I found that I was trying to crescendo as the scales went higher and higher, because I couldn't think of anything else to do. Finally out of desperation, I decided to use my 3-step method, a technique I previously had only used for main themes. (To review, the steps are: *what is the character, what in the score produces that character, and what does this imply for my interpretation?*)

It was then that I realized that I hadn't been thinking of a character at all, so it's not surprising that I was uncomfortable! Even a transition has a character. At first I couldn't describe the character, so I just thought about what I didn't like about the passage: it meanders, the texture is sparse, and it doesn't seem to be getting anywhere. It is in limbo. LIMBO! That's the character! And that was all I needed. I started thinking about how to communicate limbo in my playing. I decided that instead of trying to make a musical line where none exists, I should just **dwell in that strange moment**; I created more of a hushed sound to take the listener to another world; I stopped pushing forward and just listened to the color of the wandering passage. We do not usually think of Haydn as primarily a coloristic composer; but I have heard great pianists do beautiful, otherworldly, coloristic things with Haydn, such as taking a suddenly slower tempo in a development section in order to emphasize a strange turn of events.

So once I identify what makes me uncomfortable, it is easier to discover what it is I am fighting against, and then I can make peace with it; and now, instead of dreading that passage, I look forward to it as a place to evoke a different kind of sound.

Prokofiev, Sonata No. 2 in D Minor, Op. 14

I love Russian music, and I can hardly think of a piece that I enjoy playing more than this sonata. The beginning is passionate and driving:

Fig. 5.2. Prokofiev, Sonata No. 2 in D Minor, Op. 14, first movement, bars 1-8.

The next section is also driving, in a more percussive way:

Fig. 5.3. Prokofiev, Sonata No. 2, I, bars 9-12.

But there is one spot that always threw me. It begins at bar 16:

Fig. 5.4. Prokofiev, Sonata No. 2, I, bars 14-20.

All that energy seems to fizzle. All the fun is taken away. I found myself struggling against the sudden lack of momentum. But then I asked myself, "What am I left with, after the drive dissolves?" In other words, *how about focusing on what IS there, rather than what the passage lacks.* What I noticed then was the new ascending line in the top voice, and the melodic interest in the tenor voice.

My first step, then, should be to focus on voicing instead of bemoaning the lack of drive. That gives me something to like about the passage. I can also appreciate the importance of the pedal point on that low B octave; even though the momentum is fizzling, I can enjoy the deep sonority of the bass here; if I think in terms of orchestral colors, like a gong or low brass, I can concentrate on color rather than drive, and then I have something to communicate. So instead of fighting the fizzling energy, I can accept that "fizzling" IS the character.

Both of these examples teach me that I tend to have trouble when the music seems to lack direction. I find myself forcing the music to move forward, whereas instead I should be embracing the new features of the passage.

CHAPTER 6
Tempo

One of my students came to his lesson playing the Mozart D minor Fantasy with all the "wrong" tempi. The first Andante was ridiculously fast, and the Adagio and the Allegretto were much too slow. It was tempting to yell, "That's not how it goes!", but that probably wouldn't have been my finest hour as a teacher.

I had a split second to ask myself how I was so sure that these were the wrong tempi. That wasn't so easy to answer. So we looked at the piece together to see if we could derive the tempo directly from the score instead of from just "knowing how it goes" from tradition. **What was compelling about this process was not the actual tempi we chose, which of course are subjective, but the discovery of compositional features that helped us make the decisions.**

First, let's look at the opening Andante, and at how my student finally became convinced that he was playing it too fast.

Fig. 6.1. Mozart, Fantasy in D Minor, K. 397, bars 1-3.

Andante is a walking tempo; but Mozart also indicates cut time. In a way then, those two indications are only saying "not too fast but not too slow". How can we get more specific? *The music itself*, more than tempo indications, reveals the tempo. What is driving the opening measures forward? Nothing! In fact, the first two measures establish a meditative mood because the harmony just stays on a D minor arpeggio; there is no harmonic or melodic tension. The most interesting feature is the octave in the bass because it falls on beat two. That stopping on beat two creates a halting effect; and the fact that the octave is held makes the music sound more sustained.

Another meditative feature is the repetitive pattern of the arpeggios. Of course we can't be in a hurry if we're meditating.

There are a number of features in the next few bars that allow for some tempo flexibility, for example, the faster harmonic rhythm in bar 7. So if we want to be able to move the tempo a little starting in bar 7, we need to choose an opening tempo that's not hurried.

Fig. 6.2. Mozart, Fantasy in D Minor, bars 7-8.

Rather than trying to find the ideal tempo, our goal should be to determine a range of acceptable tempi because tempo is ultimately subjective. So what is the range for the Andante? We decided that the Andante is too fast if it does not sound meditative, and if there is no room for more movement starting in bar 7. It is too slow if it cannot be heard in cut time.

Now let's look at the Adagio:

Fig. 6.3. Mozart, Fantasy in D Minor, bars 12-15.

My student played the Adagio so slowly that the pulse was an eighth note instead of a half note. Here the question to ask is, *"What kind of music is this?"* We decided that it is opera, and in that case, the singer should be able to sing the first two bars in one breath. If she can't, then it's too slow. Also, look at the phrase structure: it's a classic antecedent/consequent group. The tempo has to move enough so the listener can hear the question and answer with continuity.

The next question is a little trickier: how do we know when the tempo for the Adagio is too *fast*? First we can ask, what is the character? We came up with "restrained passion". What made us call it "passionate"? This is the first singable melody, so that gives the piece sudden warmth; the question and answer idea creates a new urge to communicate, and the chromatic appoggiaturas add dissonance and intensity.

Secondly, what made us choose the word "restrained"? It's the sustained quality of the accompaniment: the half notes in the bass and the repeated chords. So I think that it's the accompaniment that holds back the tempo of this melody. But there is also a melodic feature that sounds restrained: those downward eighth-notes in the melody sound slow compared to the 32nds that lead into them.

Now we have our range of tempi for the Adagio: we decided that it's too slow if the singer needs a breath in the middle of the phrase; and that it feels too fast if the passage doesn't sound restrained. These may sound like fuzzy boundaries; but **while describing a character may be subjective, identifying the compositional features that create character requires objective fact-finding.**

Now let's look at the Allegretto:

Fig. 6.4. Mozart, Fantasy in D Minor, bars 55-62.

Without that allegretto marking, how would we know that this section needs to be lively, even soaring? The answer is in the rhythm: the melody features a written-in diminution that gives the illusion of accelerando:

Fig. 6.5. Mozart, Fantasy in D Minor, bars 55-58, showing motivic diminution.

The rhythmic motive is written in smaller and smaller note values as it soars upward. A pianist can show this diminution by moving the tempo forward to the top of the phrase.

We know, then, that the Allegretto is too slow if we don't get that soaring effect. I think it's too fast if we can't hear the details of the articulation. It's the articulation that makes it dancelike, rather than driven.

Grieg: Nocturne, Op. 54, No. 4

This beautiful nocturne can alternate between waltzing, floating, and soaring, but only if we pay close attention to the tempi.

Fig. 6.6. Grieg, Nocturne, Op. 54, No. 4, bars 1-7.

The opening Andante, for example, should sound like a dreamy waltz. To find a tempo we can look at the phrase-lengths for clues. The opening phrases are 2 bars long, so the tempo is too slow if those first two bars don't hold tightly together as one unit. We also know that it's too slow if the 2 against 3 sounds notey. If the tempo works, this section should sound like it's floating.

The trill section beginning in bar 15 provides another hint for tempo. The written-in accelerando is the key: if the triplet 16ths are as fast as the trill, then the tempo is too fast.

Fig. 6.7. Grieg, Nocturne, bars 15-20.

How do we know when the trill section is too slow? Notice the phrase lengths. This section from bars 15-20 is divided into two 3-bar phrases. It's too slow if we can't hear each 3-bar group hold together as a single phrase.

Now let's look at the Più mosso section. Our slowest tempo is simply whatever is slightly faster than the previous section. But what about our fastest possible tempo? This is tricky because in addition to the Più mosso marking, an accelerando is implied by the motive becoming condensed in bar 27, and even more condensed in bar 29.

Fig. 6.8. Grieg, Nocturne, bars 21-30.

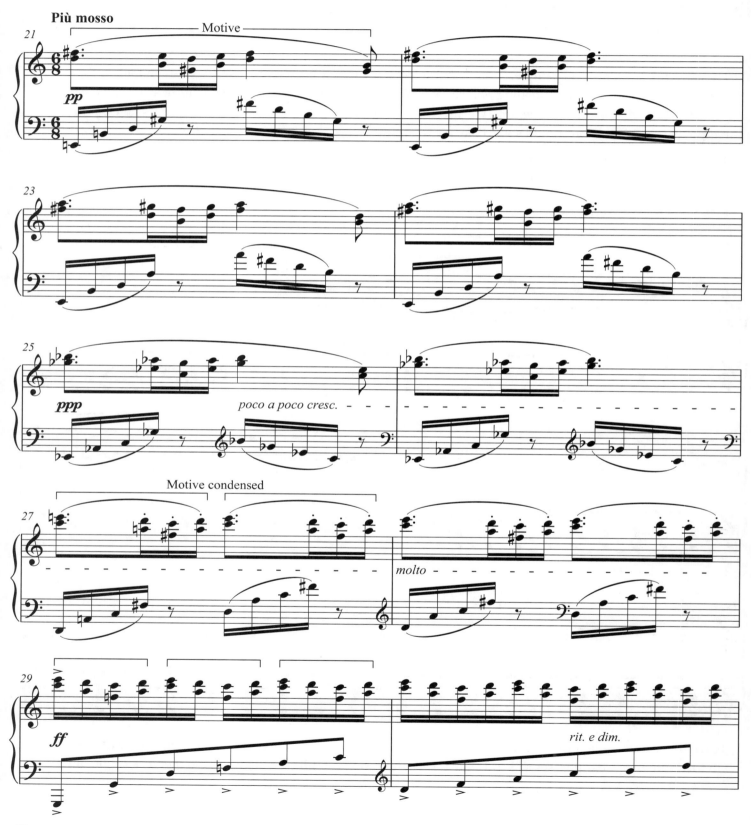

So if we decide an accelerando is coming up, we can't be at our fastest in bar 21. To clear things up we can ask, "What is the character in 21?" To me it's "soaring" because of the wide range and arching shape of the accompaniment. The harmonies also make it soar; instead of functional harmony, it is coloristic harmony: dominant 9th chords moving in parallel motion, sounding a lot like Debussy. So bar 21 needs to be fast enough that the second half of the bar soars, and faster than the previous section, but slower than bars 27-29 which need to accelerate.

Finally, what is too fast for the peak of the tempo in bars 27-29? We want this climax to be brilliant; the right hand shimmers and the left hand rings like bells. Brilliance is impossible without clarity, so it's too fast if we can't hear the rhythm of the 16ths; they have to be heard as a condensed version of the previous motive.

We have determined a range of tempi in this piece by studying texture, rhythm, range, and phrase length. If we treat a composer's tempo indication as simply a starting point, the score study that follows can get us closer to the music and to a convincing tempo.

CHAPTER 7

Which came first, the climax or the forte?

I once asked a student, "What makes this passage the climax of the piece?" Her response was "Because it says forte." *Wait a minute! It's not the climax because it says "forte"—it says "forte" because it's the climax!*

But this presents a challenge: do we really know what makes a passage the climax of a piece?

Brahms: Rhapsody in G Minor, Op. 79
The climactic passage at the end of this rhapsody provides a great example:

Fig. 7.1. Brahms, Rhapsody in G Minor, Op. 79, bars 108-116.

Many students would say that this passage is the climax because of the "big, loud chords."

What they don't realize is that the whole piece comes together here: this passage combines the striking harmony (V-VI) of the first theme with the second theme material.

Fig. 7.2. Brahms, Op. 79, first theme, bars 1-3.

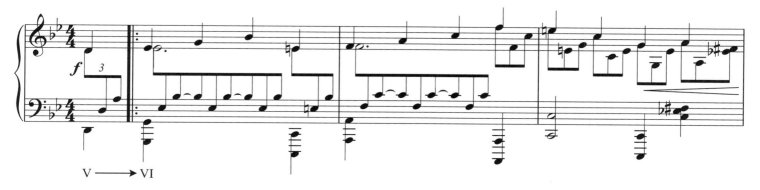

Fig. 7.3. Brahms, Op. 79, second theme, bars 21-24.

This coda is climactic because the two contrasting themes in this sonata form become unified at this moment.

Fig. 7.4. Brahms, Op. 79, coda, bar 110.

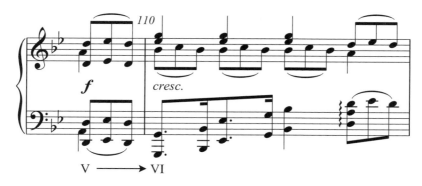

Chopin: Ballade No. 3 in A-flat, Op. 47

Here is another example of unification at a climax. Two versions of a theme come together in bar 173: The theme in F minor:

Fig. 7.5. Chopin, Ballade No. 3 in A-flat, Op. 47, bars 64-66.

And the theme in C-sharp minor:

Fig. 7.6. Chopin, Ballade, Op. 47, bars 157-158.

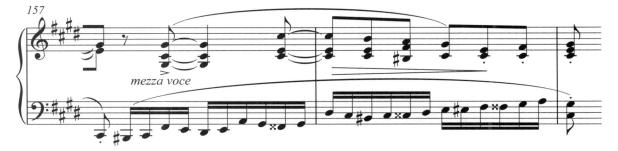

At a climactic moment (bar 173) we get the left hand chords from the F minor version, combined with the sixteenth-notes from the C-sharp minor version. Once I noticed this it seemed obvious, but when I played it in high school I was unaware of formal unity.

Fig. 7.7. Chopin, Ballade, Op. 47, bars 173-174.

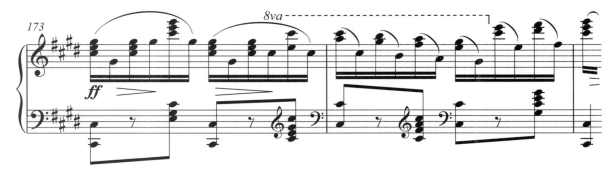

Chopin: Prelude in E Minor, Op. 28, No. 4

Sometimes it is interesting to discover what a student is observing (and not observing) about a passage.

I once asked a student what makes this passage the climax of this prelude:

Fig. 7.8. Chopin, Prelude in E Minor, Op. 28, No. 4, bars 13-18.

Her response was, "It has the highest note."

Of course that is true, but there is a lot more going on. As teachers, we can't assume that what stands out to us (the wider range and intervals, the leap to the low octave, the thicker texture, and the faster rhythm) is also clear to students. This particular student was primarily a violinist, so she was thinking linearly.

The larger impact of this passage is that in bar 16 the slow descent in the melody that we expect is interrupted, causing unexpected agitation, thereby setting up the climax with great intensity.

Grieg: Nocturne, Op. 54, No. 4

Here is an example of a passage that is climactic due largely to rhythm. We finally have the arrival on the dominant here; but the rhythmic ideas are even more compelling. The stretto effect in the right hand material is already exciting; but the biggest surprise is the augmentation of the accompaniment in bar 29:

Fig. 7.9. Grieg, Nocturne, Op. 54, No. 4, bars 27-30.

The right hand material becomes condensed and accelerated, while the left hand puts on the brakes! This tension between the two hands creates a climax of surprising intensity for this otherwise introspective piece. So if a student tells me that this passage is the climax simply because of the fortissimo marking, he will be in for an immediate lesson on score study.

PART 2

Applying the Methods
to Intermediate Repertoire

CHAPTER 8
Prokofiev Tarantella, Op. 65, No. 4
(Three-Step Method/Surprises)

This is a great teaching piece because it requires the student to project a striking contrast of moods. I will use the Three-Step method here in order to focus on character.

Fig. 8.1. Prokofiev, Tarantella, Op. 65, No. 4, bars 1-8.

Step 1: What is the character?
Ornery, stark, bold.

Step 2: What makes it ornery, stark and bold?
The material is primitive and repetitive. The opening bass notes sound stark and blunt; the texture is spare and the harmony stays in one place. In bar 5, the sudden shift to D-flat seems especially bold after those first four bars of D minor. The music sounds stubborn because *the material stays the same despite this sudden key change.* There is a single-mindedness about the expression because of the way the two hands share the material. Notice how the endings of the phrases sound clipped. It's a terse, blunt sound. This is the mechanical, motoric side of Prokofiev.

Step 3: What does this mean for my interpretation?
A stark character requires a stark sound, and for that, body language is important. Imagine a pianist moving a lot, with a look of passionate emotion trying to play this opening! The way we sit helps us get in character and affects the sound we produce. If we sit up straight without much movement, we will create a more **starchy, mechanical sound,** appropriate for this opening theme.

For the rest of the A section I will combine the 3 steps into a narrative for the sake of readability. In practice, I actually go through each passage using those steps.

Students often miss the fact that there is already a new character starting in bar 9. Suddenly it's playful. We now have melody, functional harmony and skipping rhythms. But Prokofiev keeps the texture spare, so on the page this character change is easy to miss.

Fig. 8.2. Prokofiev, Tarantella, bars 9-12.

So what does this mean for interpretation starting in bar 9? First of all, we can't sit stiffly anymore because this passage needs to swing. To communicate playfulness, the short notes need a **bouncy touch**, rather than a jab, and the new melodic line needs **dynamic shaping**.

Going into bar 21, we get one of the most energetic moments of the A section. After the opening material returns in C minor:

Fig. 8.3. Prokofiev, Tarantella, bars 17-20.

We expect it to be repeated down a half step like it was at the beginning:

Fig. 8.4. My predictable version of Prokofiev, Tarantella, bars 21-24.

But instead we get:

Fig. 8.5. Prokofiev, Tarantella, bars 21-24.

This isn't just new material; it's an augmented triad where a major triad was expected. Because we expected a major triad, the augmented triad sounds all the more unstable.

We get another surprise 4 bars later: instead of the same skipping, playful material that we expect:

Fig. 8.6. My predictable version of Prokofiev, Tarantella, bars 25-28.

we get distortion and dissonance:

Fig. 8.7. Prokofiev, Tarantella, bars 25-32.

Dissonance can be exciting, but dissonance *where we expected consonance* creates even more drama.

Notice that using the three-step method here led to a study of surprises. Once again, this shows that these methods of score study simply provide a way to begin. Each method leads to more than its title implies.

This section then, bars 21 to 32, is full of surprises and agitation. It is no longer stubborn like the opening, but instead it has urgency and drive. From the performer this calls for **shaping** that shows the rambunctious ups and downs of the line; **bringing out the melodic triplets in the bass**; and **driving to bar 32** which is the first full cadence on tonic in the piece.

Studying the lyrical middle section is a great lesson for students because of the sheer number of ways it's different from the A section. When I ask students, "what makes this middle section warm and soaring?" they usually notice only the singing melody and the melodic leaps. I have to fill in the rest: the continuity of the accompaniment; the change to the parallel major; and the smooth and stepwise bass line. They never notice that we now have 8-bar phrases instead of 4, which had been the norm for the A section; and finally, they need to be shown that the harmonic rhythm is much faster here, which makes the line surge forward.

Fig. 8.8. Prokofiev, Tarantella, middle section.

So we need some interpretive ideas to bring out these new features. We can **add pedal** for the legato; we can **bring out each new bass note** to show the faster harmonic rhythm and the smooth bass line; we need a big **swell** to show the dramatic range of the melody. And to communicate the length of the phrase we can **delay the decrescendo** as much as possible; the decrescendo should not start until after the fifth bar of each phrase so that there is no punctuation after 4 bars.

This whole 16-bar middle section is one large antecedent-consequent group. The consequent is even more glorious than the antecedent. We get a great climax in bars 44 and 45. It's not just the chromatic rise in the melody; it's the speeding up of the harmonic rhythm in bar 44 that makes this part climactic. In that measure the two sections of the piece come together—we have the two strong beats from the A section, and the linear drive of the B section at the same time. I encourage students to **broaden in bar 44** to show the chord change on the second beat and the sustained rhythm in the melody, as well as the approach to the peak of the phrase.

Let's look now at the varied return of the A section. The character here is more cryptic than ornery because of the rhythmic shift of the pitches.

Fig. 8.9. Prokofiev, Tarantella, varied return of A, bars 49-52.

A wonderful thing happens in bar 69: Prokofiev suddenly restores the rhythmic pattern, thereby creating a new surprise. In the A section this was the spot that surprised us with the augmented triad (bar 21).

Fig. 8.10. Prokofiev, Tarantella, bars 67-71.

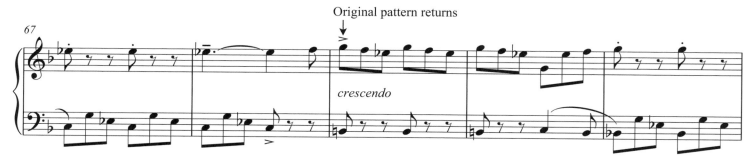

Prokofiev creates a new surprise in the same spot that there was a surprise before. In other words, the material is at once familiar and surprising.

For this varied return of A, we should **play more softly than the opening** in bar 49 in order to bring out the cryptic mood, and then **play emphatically in bar 69** to show the rhythmic surprise.

The short coda sums it all up by combining features of both sections.

Fig. 8.11. Prokofiev, Tarantella, coda.

Prokofiev takes the D major triad and the rhythm from the middle section,

Fig. 8.12. Prokofiev, Tarantella, motive from middle section, bars 33-34.

and then adds a rhythm from the A section to finish the piece.

Fig. 8.13. Prokofiev, Tarantella, motive from A section, bars 2-4.

The key to performing the coda is to **broaden** quite a bit. The ear needs time to adjust to the major mode, and to hear those ideas condensed into 4 bars.

Considering the relatively easy level of this Tarantella, it features strong characters, surprising drama, and clever compositional unity. Studying this score with a student is well worth the lesson time.

CHAPTER 9
Mozart Allegro, K. 3
(Phrase Lengths)

When a piece makes it into dozens of student collections there is usually a reason: there must be something particularly masterful about it even if it is short and easy. The charm of Mozart's Allegro, K. 3, comes largely from the phrase extensions and the subtle contrasts between the sections.

Fig. 9.1. Mozart, Allegro, K. 3.

Notice that the A section is made up of two 6-bar groups, rather than 4-bar groups. The extra bars are clearly measures 5-6 and 9-10. Imagine how it would have sounded without those measures:

Fig. 9.2. My 8-bar version of Mozart, K. 3, A section.

The original is so much more interesting! Bars 5 and 6 sound parenthetical, because they don't propel the form; and 10 and 11 add surprise because of the deceptive cadence.

So now that we recognize the beauty of the extra bars, what are we going to do interpretively? Since the action stops in bars 5 and 6, the form stands still. We can play that moment as if it is a pause in the action; in other words, softer and almost imperceptibly slower.

Next we need to communicate the surprise of the deceptive cadence. I recommend slightly broadening the first beat and eighth rest of bar 10. We can then make up that time by driving to the cadence in bars 11 and 12.

Fig. 9.3. My interpretation, Mozart, K. 3, bars 1-12.

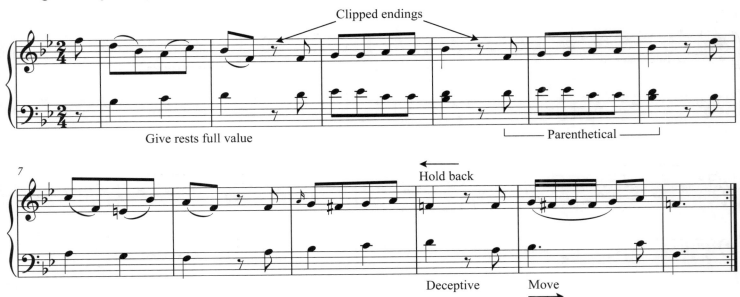

Let's look at the B section:

Fig. 9.4. Mozart, K. 3, B section.

There is a subtle change in character here. The melody is more linear and legato, whereas the opening tune kept playfully changing direction. Also, in the A section the phrases were clipped after each two bars, while in the B section a new bass line connects the phrases. Lastly, notice that B opens without any accompaniment; this absence highlights the suspended feeling of the diminished triad in the right hand, creating a contrast to the stability of the opening.

Based on these observations, I suggest the following interpretive choices: we can emphasize the clipped sound of the endings in the A section by slightly lengthening the silences. We should also show the playful ups and downs of the tune with dynamic shaping.

By contrast, in the B section I recommend playing more legato and with gradual dynamic shaping to bring out the smoother, longer line. We should avoid an accent on the downbeat of 13 to show the hovering quality of this moment compared to the stability of the opening. Finally, If we bring out the left hand line where it connects the phrases (bars 14 and 18), we can further emphasize the linear texture.

Let's look at the ending:

Fig. 9.5. Mozart, K. 3, bars 21-30.

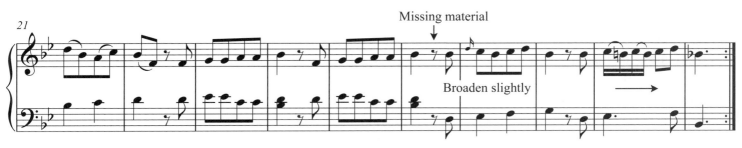

The return of the A section is the same as the opening until the last 4 bars. Mozart skips 2 measures between 26 and 27 so that the return of A is 2 bars shorter. Instead of what we heard in bars 7 and 8, he skips to the deceptive cadence. We *must* show this surprise in performance! How we do it is probably less important than that we do *something*. I suggest broadening slightly in 27 and 28 to show that this is unexpected material. Then we can balance this broadening by driving to the end in the last two measures.

To reiterate a comment from the introduction to this book, it is possible for a good musician to play this way instinctively, before studying the score. But in order to *teach* the piece well, we must be able to point out these interesting features, so that the student understands the reasons for our interpretive suggestions.

CHAPTER 10
Beethoven Sonatina in G
(Surprises/Phrase Length)

The surprises in this sonatina are easy to miss because the piece is so familiar. True confessions: I missed the most obvious one.

There are several surprises in bars 5 and 6, and in order to get students to notice them I always ask, "Why do you think Beethoven wrote a crescendo there?"

Fig. 10.1. Beethoven, Sonatina in G, Anh. 5, first movement, bars 1-8.

I hope they will notice the F natural and the longer phrase length. But it wasn't until I made a conscious decision to study the score that I noticed the most obvious surprise: that in bar 5 into 6 the melody *rises* at the end of the slur. Realizing that I had missed this reminded me that familiar music needs score study because it is so easy to take the surprises for granted.

The surprises in the middle section beginning in bar 9 are all about phrase length. Instead of two shorts and then a long, we get the shortest phrases in the middle of the section:

Fig. 10.2. Beethoven, Sonatina in G, I, bars 9-18.

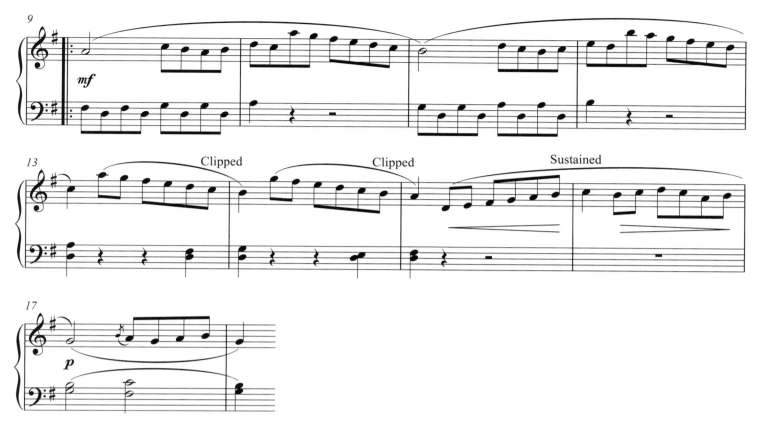

I tell my students that we can't just keep plowing forward through the phrases that are suddenly short (13 and 14). The fact that those 1-bar phrases end on quarter notes instead of half notes means that they are meant to sound clipped. Also with the unexpected chords (as opposed to flowing eighths) in the left hand Beethoven is clearly putting on the brakes. What does this mean for interpretation? I think we must move forward in 9 through 12 to show the flowing texture; then play the next short phrases with clipped endings, and let the left hand chords create a halting effect. Then, when the bottom drops out in 15, we can play freely as if this were a miniature cadenza. We can emphasize the continuity of this two-bar phrase by getting a singing tone on the quarter note downbeat of bar 16.

The beauty of the coda is not in the melodic material or the harmony; it is all very simple and diatonic.

Fig. 10.3. Beethoven, Sonatina in G, I, bars 25-34.

What is beautiful is the texture and phrase length: we finally have long phrases with a continuous legato. Our main job interpretively is to communicate long legato phrases. We can do that by shaping the arpeggiated melody with a swell, and by making the accompaniment as smooth as possible. The final chords can be played simply, because a ritardando is already written in with an increase of note values from quarter note, half, to whole.

CHAPTER 11
Gurlitt Etude, Op. 82, No. 65
(Favorite Part Method)

It's hard to find exciting romantic pieces for this early intermediate level. That's why this etude has found its way into so many collections.

Fig. 11.1. Gurlitt, Etude, Op. 82, No. 65.

In 19 fleeting measures, Gurlitt takes us on a fervent and mysterious journey in the spirit of Schubert lieder. Teaching this etude gives us a chance to share some of the darker Schubert songs with the student, particularly "Aufenthalt" (*Dwelling*), which has a strikingly similar mood and texture to the Gurlitt:

Fig. 11.2. Schubert, Aufenthalt, bars 1-14.

A short piece like this Gurlitt etude is fertile ground for the "Favorite Part" method. Due to its economy of musical material, we can quickly see how one expressive passage relates to the piece as a whole.

My favorite part is the climax in bars 14 and 15. At first glance it might seem that the beauty of this moment lies in the series of suspensions in the right hand. But it turns out that the material in the left hand is just as important, and that this moment is inevitable because of the preceding surprises in bars 11 and 12.

The piece begins with a four bar phrase in D minor. The next phrase is parallel to the first, ending this time in F major with the same cadential motive as in the first phrase. But the phrase that follows is cut short in bar 11, omitting the cadential motive we expect in the melody. The other surprise happens in the right hand accompaniment: the chord doesn't change in bar 12, but hovers instead for much longer than we expect. When we finally get the cadential motive (fragmented) in bar 13, Gurlitt prolongs this fulfilling moment with the beautiful sequence in bars 14 and 15, the heart of the piece. He also extends the last note of the motive to a dotted half note:

Fig. 11.3. Gurlitt, Etude, bars 14-15.

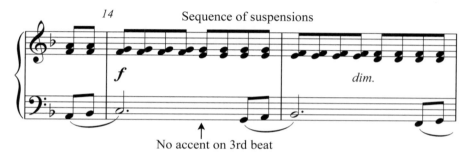

These dotted half notes create a soaring effect, changing the pulse to one large beat per bar for measures 14 and 15. The bass note we expected on beat three is missing, and its absence gives the beautiful suspensions in the right hand more prominence. This is a climax of wonderful sweep and inevitability, especially for such a miniature work.

Asking the question, "What makes this my favorite part?" can lead to uncovering the magic of a piece. In this case, the answer was in the surprises, and the musical resolution of those surprises. Of course, we spend much of the lesson time helping students with the technique of balance between the hands; but it only takes a minute or two to present these ideas, and finding the magic is what makes the technical work worth the effort.

CHAPTER 12
Mozart Minuet, K. 1
(Phrase Length/Surprises)

Mozart wrote this little piece when he was only a child, but it already shows his genius.

Fig. 12.1. Mozart, Minuet, K. 1.

Two aspects of this piece particularly interest me; the variety of texture and rhythm, and the contrasts between the minuet and the trio. The beauty of the opening is the change in bar 5 from simple parallel tenths to counterpoint, and from a simple rhythm to hemiola. To show this change from simple to more complex, we can give tone and direction to the new bass line in bar 5 to show its importance, and to emphasize this longer, more active phrase.

Fig. 12.2. Mozart, K. 1, bars 1-8.

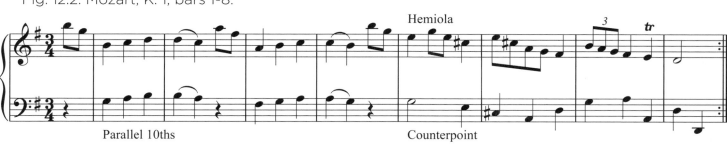

When the first phrase is repeated, it sounds even more sweet and simple after we have heard bars 5-8. This contrast gives us a hint for dynamics: the opening has to be softer than the next 4 bars, especially at the repeat.

Perhaps the loveliest spot in the piece is the opening of the trio.

Fig. 12.3. Mozart, K. 1, bars 14-25.

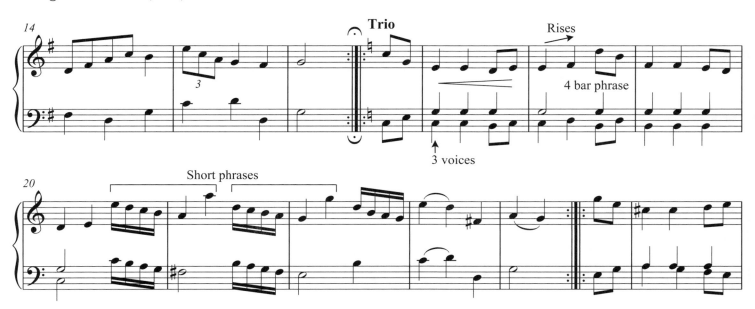

The warmth of new subdominant key, combined with the thicker texture creates a surprisingly rich sound. A third voice joins in creating more of a chamber music atmosphere. By adding weight (another voice) to the eighth note pick-ups, Mozart equalizes the three beats in the measure, creating a new, more sustained sound.

The changes in the melody are just as striking. In the first bar of the trio, notice that the second beat stays on the same pitch (E) rather than rising as it does in the minuet. Add to that the richer texture and we get a more sustained sound. Any good string trio would choose a more legato bowing here, so I add a touch of pedal to imitate that kind of string playing.

Another surprise is that the melody **rises** on the second beat of bar 18, instead of falling as it does in the minuet. The surprising note that rises is F natural, the note on which the key change depends. I think it makes artistic sense not to taper to the F. If we sustain the sound instead of tapering, we can show that this is a four-bar, rather than a two-bar phrase.

Finally, notice that as the trio continues, the phrase lengths continue to be different from the minuet. The following example shows the piece with my phrase markings:

Fig. 12.4. Mozart, K. 1, showing phrase structure.

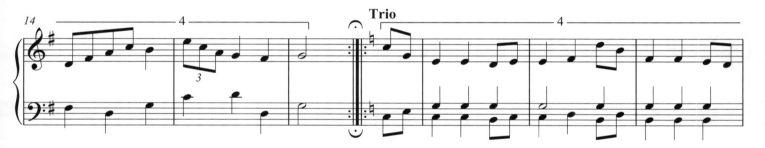

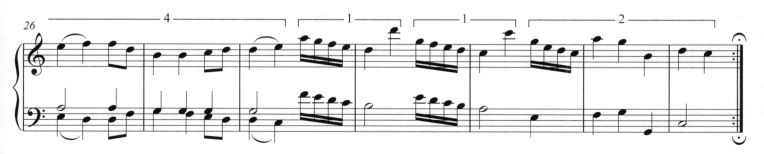

It seems that the graceful, lighter moments happen in short phrases, while the linear and more legato passages coincide with the longer phrases. The fact that the minuet and trio have opposite phrase structures makes the contrasts between the sections discussed above all the more striking.

CHAPTER 13
Burgmüller Arabesque, Op. 100, No. 2
(Surprises)

Practically every student plays this piece! It is masterfully crafted, and so much more appealing than a typical etude. It is full of surprises, and there is something to appreciate compositionally in every line.

Fig. 13.1. Burgmüller, Arabesque, Op. 100, No. 2.

The first surprise happens in measure 5: the melodic pattern skips the material we expect. Instead of continuing the pattern predictably:

Fig. 13.2. My predictable version of Burgmüller, Arabesque, bars 3-6.

Burgmüller skips ahead:

Fig. 13.3. Burgmüller, Arabesque, bars 3-6.

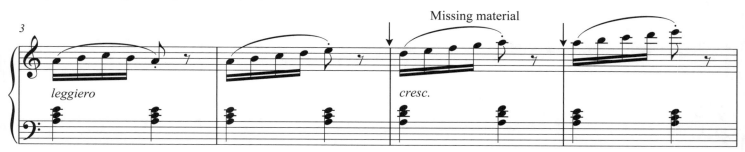

By skipping material Burgmüller creates a sense of rushing to the top of the phrase. For performance, then, I suggest opening the piece with a very strict tempo, and then in bars 5 and 6 moving the phrase forward to show the accelerated material.

The next surprise happens in measure 7. Suddenly the theme becomes lyrical and moves abruptly to C Major. The way the piece begins, with the scherzando quality of the runs, we don't expect this opening phrase group to end so lyrically. Imagine this piece as a simpler, more banal etude:

Fig. 13.4. My banal version of Burgmüller, Arabesque, opening.

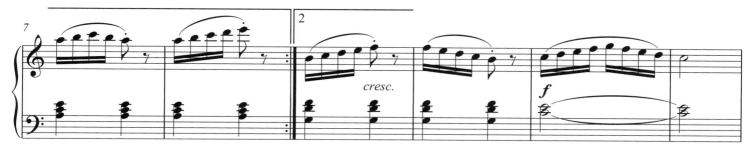

Besides omitting the lyrical phrase, this banal version leaves out an important rhythmic feature: Burgmüller puts the strong beat on the beginning of each measure until bar 7; then the emphasis shifts to the middle of the bar, culminating in the strong accent on beat 2 of the first ending:

Fig. 13.5. Burgmüller, Arabesque, bars 1-11.

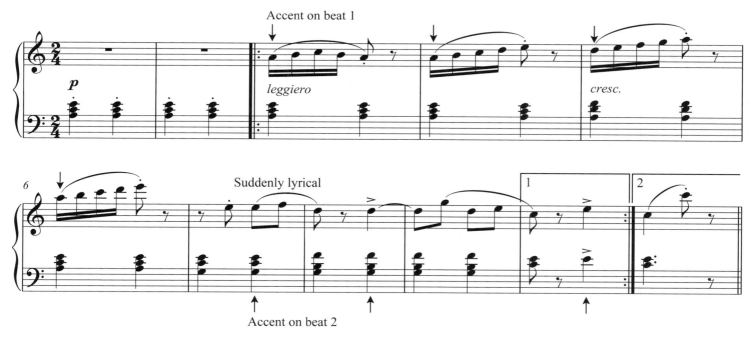

I encourage my students to make a big deal out of the surprising change in bar 7. I even suggest adding touches of pedal there to show the shift to a sweeter mood. I also recommend taking a little time on the downbeat of bar 7 to emphasize the sudden changes.

I think the beauty of the B section is that Burgmüller combines the two characters of the A section: we get the lyricism in the right hand and the 16ths in the left hand at the same time.

Fig. 13.6. Burgmüller, Arabesque, bars 12-15.

That's already clever; he could have simply reversed the texture of the A section:

Fig. 13.7. My predictable version of Burgmüller, Arabesque, bars 12-13.

But there's something even more subtle to appreciate: the first four notes in the right hand in bars 12 and 13 form an augmented version of the last motive of the A section:

Fig. 13.8. Burgmüller, Arabesque, thematic unity, bars 9-13.

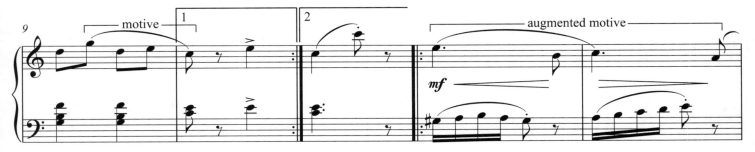

This kind of thematic unity makes the piece more convincing, even though the listener is probably not conscious of it.

The end of the B section is also surprising: in bars 18 and 19 the texture melts into lyrical, parallel 6ths.

Fig. 13. 9. Burgmüller, Arabesque, bars 16-20.

Lyrical parallel 6ths

Burgmüller could have simply continued the same material there:

Fig. 13.10. My predictable version of Burgmüller, Arabesque, bars 16-20.

So, of course, I encourage students to show this change of pattern in bar 18 by taking time and playing with a more lyrical sound.

Let's look at what happens when the A section returns. Again we get a surprise in the 5th bar of the theme (bar 24), but it is a different surprise. Not only do we stay in A minor instead of going to C Major, but both the melody and harmony are different than we expect with a pedal point underneath:

Fig. 13.11. Burgmüller, Arabesque, bars 24-27.

A lesser composer might have just written a literal transposition to A minor of bars 7-10:

Fig. 13.12. My predictable version of Burgmüller, Arabesque, bars 24-27.

But in bar 24, Burgmüller gives us a poignant dissonance, right where we expected the happy C Major chord. I always encourage students to do something to show these surprises, particularly to take a little time on the downbeat of 24.

Even the brief coda is distinctive and unpredictable.

Fig. 13.13. Burgmüller, Arabesque, Coda.

Notice that Burgmüller skips the second bar that we expect from the beginning; bar 29 goes to the subdominant when we expect another bar of tonic. That sets an accelerando in motion because the harmonic rhythm is suddenly twice as fast as we expect, and the pitches climb faster. The last two bars are very exciting because first of all, the 16ths *descend* a fifth for the first and only time in the piece; it is also the only time we get 16ths in both hands; and finally, there is a big jump down in register, suddenly interrupting the ascending runs. So bar 32 makes a big statement and jumps out of the context, and therefore I think we have to do something dramatic and daring there. I recommend pushing the tempo forward beginning in 29, and taking a slight breath before the downward scale in 32 to show that the upward momentum has been cut off. That breath will emphasize the interruption and declamatory character of the last two bars.

The coda is also the only phrase in the piece that is **6** bars long: 4+2. That asymmetry adds to the unpredictability of the ending, and gives us another reason to be daringly dramatic at the end.

CHAPTER 14
Haydn Allegro in F Major, Hob. XVII: Anh.
(Surprises/Structural Unity)

This piece, as short as it is, has the wit, surprise and drama we expect from Haydn. It also sounds like one of his scampering string quartet movements, in which the first violinist leads with lightning speed, while the lower voices accompany lightly, jumping at the chance to play the tune in those rare moments that it shows up in their part. (An extended version of this piece can be found in one of Haydn's quartets: opus 74, no. 2.)

The piece opens with two phrases that would be parallel except for the surprise at the end of the second phrase, in which he reverses the rhythm that we expect:

Fig. 14.1. Haydn, Allegro in F Major, Hob. XVII: Anh., bars 1-8.

The sixteenths in the second phrase come *before* the last measure. A lesser composer might have simply written a second phrase parallel to the first:

Fig. 14.2. My predictable version of Haydn, Allegro in F, bars 5-8.

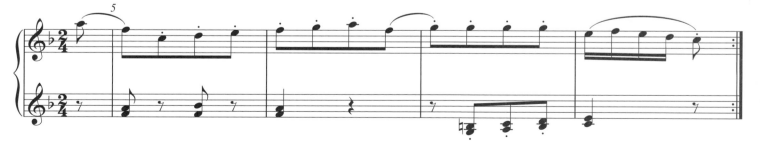

By reversing the rhythm, Haydn gives the whole phrase group a witty unpredictability.

The second distinctive feature of this opening is the blending of melody and accompaniment. Notice how the left hand in bar 3 is thematic:

Fig. 14.3. Haydn, Allegro in F, bars 1-4.

He could have just continued the simple accompaniment:

Fig. 14.4. My predictable version of Haydn, Allegro in F, bars 3-4.

By incorporating the thematic eighths, Haydn not only unifies the melody and accompaniment, but also creates a momentum that propels the phrase to the cadence. That makes the mood rambunctious and playful.

The idea of unifying the melody and accompaniment by making the accompaniment thematic is a trait we see in Haydn's sophisticated later works, such as the last movement of the C Major Sonata, Hob. 50:

Fig. 14.5. Haydn, Sonata in C, Hob. XVI/50, III, bars 1-7.

In this theme the accompaniment actually has the motive *first*.

Let's return to the Allegro in F. The following excerpt shows some interpretive ideas for performance, based on my observations about the blended texture and the rhythmic surprise:

Fig. 14.6. My interpretation, Haydn, Allegro in F, bars 1-8.

We can bring out the left hand motive in bar 3 with a swell because it's thematic. To show the contrast in rhythm of the two phrases we can crescendo into bar 4, emphasizing the momentum of the left hand, and decrescendo into bar 8, accenting the early sixteenths. I recommend playing the last two bars of each phrase with an increased sense of momentum. Even body language can help us feel this; we can sit straight and relatively still for the first two bars of each phrase, and then move more as the momentum increases.

Let's look at the B section, beginning with bars 9-12.

Fig. 14.7. Haydn, Allegro in F, bars 9-12:

At first glance it is just a harmonic sequence; but there is more going on here. Notice that the outer voices have the motive from the first section in contrary motion. This means we must not treat the left hand as an accompaniment, but as a chamber music partner to the other voices, like the cellist in a quartet. This section is more declamatory than the opening because now all voices are moving in the same rhythm, and are less subservient to the first violinist.

But the next phrase group going into 13 is very different:

Fig. 14.8. Haydn, Allegro in F, bars 13-16.

We have just had a harmonic sequence that moved pretty quickly; but now we are on a plateau: the piece seems to be standing still harmonically and melodically. If we respond to that by playing 13-16 objectively, as if it were parenthetical, then we can be expressive when we get to that beautiful measure 17:

Fig. 14.9. Haydn, Allegro in F, bars 17-21.

Here not only do we get a modulation, but it's suddenly lyrical, and in the accompaniment we have sustained chords for the first time. I take time here and look for a warmer sound.

The next passage is a transition back to the A section material. The piece is suspended on a dominant seventh:

Fig. 14.10. Haydn, Allegro in F, bars 21-26.

so I suggest making this passage hover rather than move with any direction, until we get to 25. Even the most inexperienced student can hear, when we point it out, that bars 25 and 26 compress that 2-note slur material. This stretto idea is so easy to see that I like to get the *student* to figure out what's happening (with some leading questions) and get *them* to suggest moving forward there.

What is most interesting about the return of the A section is the rhythmic surprise at the end of this second phrase—a sudden silence:

Fig. 14.11. Haydn, Allegro in F, bars 27-35.

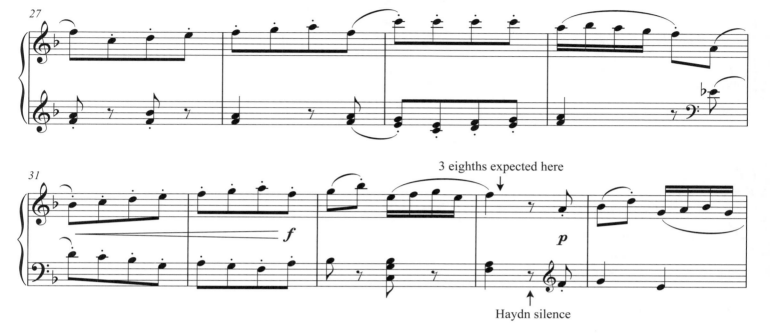

We expect three eighths instead of a quarter note and a rest:

Fig. 14.12. My predictable version of Haydn, Allegro in F, bars 33-34, melody.

That rest wouldn't be so noticeable if the three eighths weren't expected. But since the rest is unexpected it becomes a *Haydn silence*. In other words, this is one of Haydn's special silences that he used for punctuation, drama, suspense, or as in this case, humor. I like to take a little extra time on these rests.

The beauty of the coda is that the A and B sections blend together; starting in 38 we get the texture of the B section in the right hand, and the motive of the A section in the left hand.

Fig. 14.13. Haydn, Allegro in F, bars 36-44.

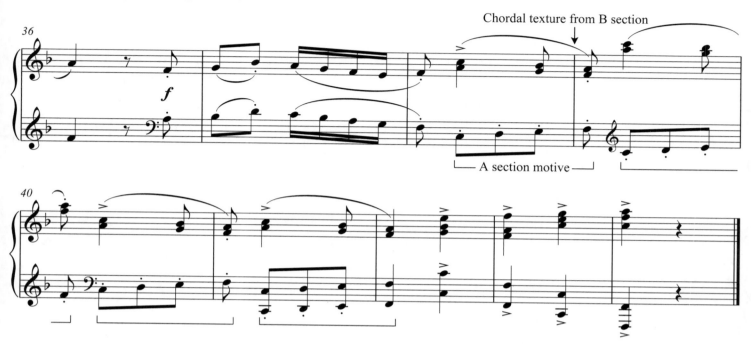

In fact, Haydn is so intent on revisiting that motive that we hear it over and over and finally in octaves for emphasis.

I've always wanted a big sound from my students in the last four chords but only recently did I realize that these chords are particularly emphatic because the tune in the soprano voice is a motive from the B section in disguise:

Fig. 14.14. Haydn, Allegro in F, motivic relationship between bars 11-12 and 42-44.

So considering this is a short student piece, if it is played with attention to these structural features, we get a taste of the boldness and excitement of some of Haydn's great sonatas and quartets.

CHAPTER 15
Burgmüller Ballade, Op. 100, No. 15
("What kind of music is this?"/Tempo)

Burgmüller was a master of imitating different styles. Some of his pieces show influence of Mendelssohn and Schumann; others sound like Gilbert and Sullivan. The stormy opening section of this ballade comes right out of melodramatic Wagner opera, specifically the Flying Dutchman which was written a few years earlier. I recommend that a student learning this piece listen to the opening bars of the overture, in which the orchestra imitates the sound of howling winds at sea. In the opening of the Ballade, the swirling left hand sixteenths take the role of the wind, and the sforzandi sound like Wagner's trumpet warning calls.

Fig. 15.1. Burgmüller, Ballade, Op. 100, No. 15, bars 1-30.

Flowing rhythm

My decision to imitate opera affects my choice of tempo. If those sixteenths represent wind they must be fast enough to sound swirling, rather than notey. The opening chords should create a soft spooky texture in a pulse of one, rather than drawing the listener's attention to each individual chord. To do the piece justice, it should only be assigned to students who are advanced enough to play it at sufficient speed.

The same holds true for the lovely middle section starting in bar 23; this soaring melody would most likely be conducted in a large four pattern, one measure getting one beat. If it retains the smaller pulse of the A section it will lose its flow. But *how do we know* this middle section needs to flow? The most obvious answer is the new linear and legato melody; but there are more subtle reasons: first of all, the left hand chords of the middle section come *after* the downbeat, flowing into the next bar:

Fig. 15.2. Burgmüller, Ballade, bars 23-26.

Whereas the chords in the A section began on the downbeat followed by a rest, creating a halting effect:

Fig. 15.3. Burgmüller, Ballade, bars 11-14.

There is another important reason to move the tempo forward in 23. Notice the motivic relationship: the first appearance of this motive outlines the dissonant interval of a seventh.

Fig. 15.4. Burgmüller, Ballade, bars 11-14.

Then in the B section the motive soars joyfully up to an octave.

Fig. 15.5. Burgmüller, Ballade, bars 23-26.

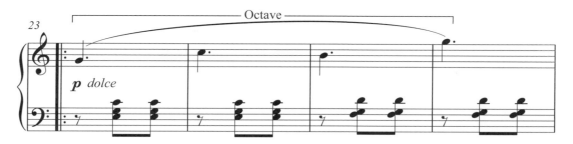

The fact that these two opposite characters share the same tune invites the performer to show this thematic transformation by contrasting them as much as possible.

To get inside this piece, asking the question, "What kind of music is this?" led to a discussion of operatic style, programmatic elements and tempo. In the tempo discussion, we compared the A and B sections, and that comparison led to observations about rhythmic texture and thematic transformation. Although students at a Burgmüller level are not equipped to do this kind of analysis, I have found that they can easily appreciate it if I demonstrate at the piano. It only takes a few minutes of the lesson. Admittedly, score study does present some work for the teacher outside of the lesson, but it is especially worthwhile with pieces we assign often. Moreover, the more often we delve into the music, the less time it takes to find magic.

FINAL THOUGHTS

I am learning that studying the score is a conscious decision. Even after writing this book I still consciously have to decide to study the score. Otherwise I find myself just practicing technical passages or using musical instinct only.

It can be intimidating to begin a score study session; this is such great music, who am I to think I can analyze it? *What if this time I don't discover anything?* These are the times when I should heed the advice of my former teacher, Gyorgy Sebok: "Look at a page of the score and list everything you see."

It's right before your eyes.

SCHIRMER
PERFORMANCE EDITIONS
BOOK ONLY EDITIONS

Pedagogical in nature, these editions offer insightful interpretive suggestions, pertinent fingering, and historical and stylistic commentary.

The book with audio versions remain available as well, priced slightly higher.
Visit **halleonard.com** to see a listing of all book/audio versions available.

J.S. BACH: FIRST LESSONS IN BACH
ed. Christos Tsitsaros
00297090........................ $9.99

J.S. BACH: TWO-PART INVENTIONS
ed. Christopher Taylor
00297091........................ $7.99

J. FRIEDRICH BURGMÜLLER: 25 PROGRESSIVE STUDIES, OP. 100
ed. Margaret Otwell
00297086.......................... 7.99

FREDERIC CHOPIN: PRELUDES
ed. Brian Ganz
00297085........................ $9.99

MUZIO CLEMENTI: SONATINAS, OP. 36
ed. Jennifer Linn
00297087........................ $7.99

CARL CZERNY: PRACTICAL METHOD FOR BEGINNERS, OP. 599
ed. Matthew Edwards
00297083........................ $9.99

CARL CZERNY: SCHOOL OF VELOCITY, OP. 299
ed. Matthew Edwards
00297084........................ $8.99

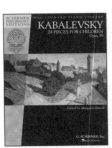

DMITRI KABALEVSKY: 24 PIECES FOR CHILDREN OP. 39
ed. Margaret Otwell
00297092........................ $10.99

W.A. MOZART: 15 EASY PIANO PIECES
ed. Elena Abend
00297088........................ $7.99

ERIK SATIE: GYMNOPEDIES AND GNOSSIENNES
ed. Matthew Edwards
00297089........................ $7.99

THE 20TH CENTURY — ELEMENTARY LEVEL
compiled and edited by Richard Walters
00297094........................ $9.99

THE 20TH CENTURY – INTERMEDIATE LEVEL
compiled and edited by Richard Walters
00297097........................ $10.99

G. SCHIRMER, Inc.

FOR MORE INFORMATION, SEE YOUR LOCAL MUSIC DEALER,
OR WRITE TO:

HAL•LEONARD®
CORPORATION
7777 W. BLUEMOUND RD. P.O. BOX 13819 MILWAUKEE, WI 53213

Prices, contents and availability subject to change without notice.

0115

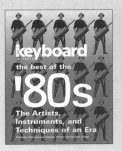

COMPOSER SHOWCASE
HAL LEONARD STUDENT PIANO LIBRARY

This series showcases great original piano music from our **Hal Leonard Student Piano Library** family of composers, including Bill Boyd, Phillip Keveren, Carol Klose, Jennifer Linn, Mona Rejino, Eugénie Rocherolle and more. Carefully graded for easy selection, each book contains gems that are certain to become tomorrow's classics!

BILL BOYD

JAZZ BITS (AND PIECES)
Early Intermediate Level
00290312 11 Solos......................$7.99

JAZZ DELIGHTS
Intermediate Level
00240435 11 Solos......................$7.99

JAZZ FEST
Intermediate Level
00240436 10 Solos......................$7.99

JAZZ PRELIMS
Early Elementary Level
00290032 12 Solos......................$6.99

JAZZ SKETCHES
Intermediate Level
00220001 8 Solos........................$7.99

JAZZ STARTERS
Elementary Level
00290425 10 Solos......................$7.99

JAZZ STARTERS II
Late Elementary Level
00290434 11 Solos......................$7.99

JAZZ STARTERS III
Late Elementary Level
00290465 12 Solos......................$7.99

THINK JAZZ!
Early Intermediate Level
00290417 Method Book $10.99

TONY CARAMIA

JAZZ MOODS
Intermediate Level
00296728 8 Solos........................$6.95

SUITE DREAMS
Intermediate Level
00296775 4 Solos........................$6.99

SONDRA CLARK

DAKOTA DAYS
Intermediate Level
00296521 5 Solos........................$6.95

FAVORITE CAROLS FOR TWO
Intermediate Level
00296530 5 Duets.......................$7.99

FLORIDA FANTASY SUITE
Intermediate Level
00296766 3 Duets.......................$7.95

ISLAND DELIGHTS
Intermediate Level
00296666 4 Solos........................$6.95

THREE ODD METERS
Intermediate Level
00296472 3 Duets.......................$6.95

MATTHEW EDWARDS

CONCERTO FOR YOUNG PIANISTS
for 2 Pianos, Four Hands
Intermediate Level Book/CD
00296356 3 Movements..................$16.95

CONCERTO NO. 2 IN G MAJOR
For 2 Pianos, 4 Hands
Intermediate Level Book/CD
00296670 3 Movements..................$16.95

PHILLIP KEVEREN

MOUSE ON A MIRROR
Late Elementary Level
00296361 5 Solos........................$6.95

MUSICAL MOODS
Elementary/Late Elementary Level
00296714 7 Solos........................$5.95

SHIFTY-EYED BLUES
Late Elementary Level
00296374 5 Solos........................$6.99

TEX-MEX REX
Late Elementary Level
00296353 6 Solos........................$6.99

CAROL KLOSE

CORAL REEF SUITE
Late Elementary Level
00296354 7 Solos........................$6.99

DESERT SUITE
Intermediate Level
00296667 6 Solos........................$7.99

FANCIFUL WALTZES
Early Intermediate Level
00296473 5 Solos........................$7.95

GARDEN TREASURES
Late Intermediate Level
00296787 5 Solos........................$7.99

ROMANTIC EXPRESSIONS
Intermediate/Late Intermediate Level
00296923 5 Solos........................$8.99

WATERCOLOR MINIATURES
Early Intermediate Level
00296848 7 Solos........................$7.99

JENNIFER LINN

AMERICAN IMPRESSIONS
Intermediate Level
00296471 6 Solos........................$7.99

CHRISTMAS IMPRESSIONS
Intermediate Level
00296706 8 Solos........................$7.99

JUST PINK
Elementary Level
00296722 9 Solos........................$6.99

LES PETITES IMAGES
Late Elementary Level
00296664 7 Solos........................$7.99

LES PETITES IMPRESSIONS
Intermediate Level
00296355 6 Solos........................$7.99

REFLECTIONS
Late Intermediate Level
00296843 5 Solos........................$7.99

TALES OF MYSTERY
Intermediate Level
00296769 6 Solos........................$8.99

MONA REJINO

CIRCUS SUITE
Late Elementary Level
00296665 5 Solos........................$5.95

JUST FOR KIDS
Elementary Level
00296840 8 Solos........................$7.99

MERRY CHRISTMAS MEDLEYS
Intermediate Level
00296799 5 Solos........................$7.99

PORTRAITS IN STYLE
Early Intermediate Level
00296507 6 Solos........................$7.99

EUGÉNIE ROCHEROLLE

ENCANTOS ESPAÑOLES (SPANISH DELIGHTS)
Intermediate Level
00125451 6 Solos........................$7.99

JAMBALAYA
For 2 Pianos, 8 Hands
Intermediate Level
00296654 Piano Ensemble.............$9.99

JAMBALAYA
For 2 Pianos, 4 Hands
Intermediate Level
00296725 Piano Duo (2 Pianos)......$7.95

TOUR FOR TWO
Late Elementary Level
00296832 6 Duets.......................$7.99

TREASURES
Late Elementary/Early Intermediate Level
00296924 7 Solos........................$8.99

CHRISTOS TSITSAROS

DANCES FROM AROUND THE WORLD
Early Intermediate Level
00296688 7 Solos........................$6.95

LYRIC BALLADS
Intermediate/Late Intermediate Level
00102404 6 Solos........................$8.99

POETIC MOMENTS
Intermediate Level
00296403 8 Solos........................$8.99

SONATINA HUMORESQUE
Late Intermediate Level
00296772 3 Movements.................$6.99

SONGS WITHOUT WORDS
Intermediate Level
00296506 9 Solos........................$7.95

THREE PRELUDES
Early Advanced Level
00130747 ....$8.99

THROUGHOUT THE YEAR
Late Elementary Level
00296723 12 Duets......................$6.95

ADDITIONAL COLLECTIONS

ALASKA SKETCHES
by Lynda Lybeck-Robinson
Early Intermediate Level
00119637 8 Solos........................$7.99

AMERICAN PORTRAITS
by Wendy Stevens
Intermediate Level
00296817 6 Solos........................$7.99

AN AWESOME ADVENTURE
by Lynda Lybeck-Robinson
Late Elementary Level
00137563.................................$7.99

AT THE LAKE
by Elvina Pearce
Elementary/Late Elementary Level
00131642 10 Solos and Duets.........$7.99

COUNTY RAGTIME FESTIVAL
by Fred Kern
Intermediate Level
00296882 7 Rags........................$7.99

PLAY THE BLUES!
by Luann Carman (Method Book)
Early Intermediate Level
00296357 10 Solos......................$9.99

7777 W. BLUEMOUND RD. P.O. BOX 13819 MILWAUKEE, WI 53213